A Question of Gravity and Light

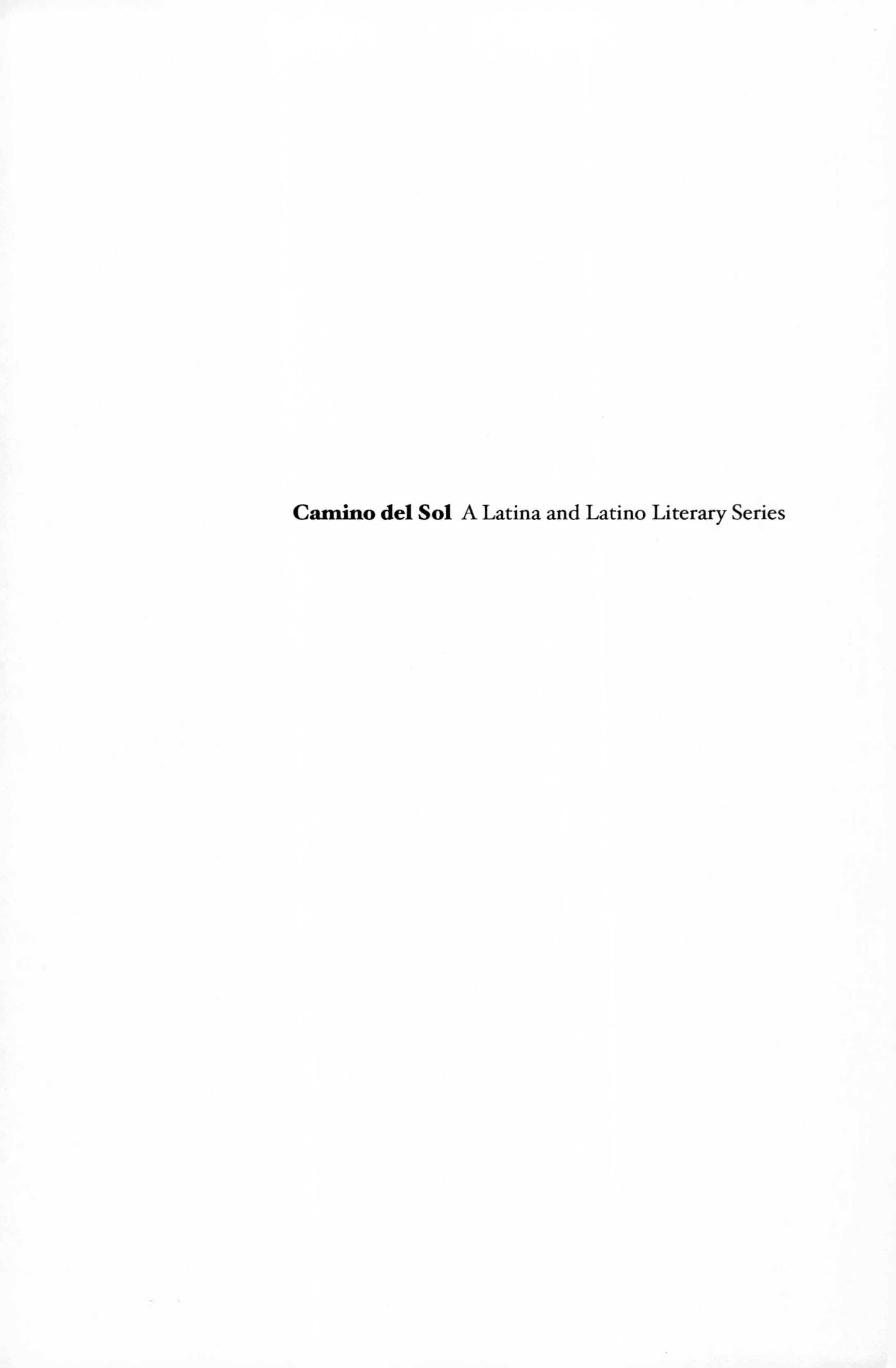

Camino del Sol A Latina and Latino Literary Series

A Question of Gravity and Light

Blas Falconer

The University of Arizona Press
Tucson

The University of Arizona Press

Library of Congress Cataloging-in-Publication Data
Falconer, Blas.
A question of gravity and light / Blas Falconer.
p. cm. — (Camino del sol)
ISBN-13: 978-0-8165-2622-2 (pbk. : acid-free paper)
ISBN-10: 0-8165-2622-2 (pbk. : acid-free paper)
I. Title.
PS3606.A425Q47 2007
811'.6—dc22 2006036413

Publication of this book is made possible in part by the proceeds of a permanent endowment created with the assistance of a Challenge Grant from the National Endowment for the Humanities, a federal agency.

Manufactured in the United States of America on acid-free, archival-quality paper.

12 11 10 09 08 07 6 5 4 3 2 1

For Carmen Buono

Contents

A Question of Gravity and Light

Dead Reckoning

The morning woke up dark and tired. Horses walked
in figure eights beneath the trees. The sky had crawled
south-southwest all night. The ferry left at six,
bells marked the hour, and everyone was counting.

You shuffled on. You took what you could carry.
A couple leaned against the rail, kissed, his hand
up her shirt, while others looked ahead. You thought,
The statue of St. Christopher, the wooden boy in his arms,

the bone encased in glass. The sea was calm. You thought
you saw the lights. They had said, *Blue houses on*
the mountainside. They had said, *On every roof, tins to catch*
the rain. You thought the boat would take you there.

The Given Account

Puerto Rico, 1510

They said they were gods, and we believed—
they crossed uncrossable seas, after all,

in ships with sails like wings—but Salcedo
is dead. Pacing river shallows, turning rocks,

sifting sand for flecks of gold, he cut his foot
on stone or shell, sending braids of blood

downstream. Overhead, wind shook trees
so leaves and light spilled in, catching a school

of fish, a silver shimmer. I was there.
Kneeling on the bank, I dressed his wound,

pressing strips of cloth to stop the flood,
but red spots seeped through the weave,

my fingers wet with blood, his blood,
no different from mine. He winced, his face

paled by pain, but nothing, nothing changed,
no dove, no cloud, no beam of light, and he

a god or son of god? I, who came to drink,
struck dumb by one thought—they bleed, they die—

led him back into the pool and pushed
his head below. His arms thrashed, legs kicked,

lungs inhaled mouths of water. He stopped.
Three days I stayed to see him stir, but he,

not strongest, weakest, or cruelest of them,
did not move. I pulled him out. He hung

wet and limp and heavy in my arms—
this man, this man, almost too much to bear.

Lament

You wondered how you'd gotten here. The day began,
prying wedges from a bright yellow rind,
and ended, closing a door on a field of fireflies.
Outside it was already summer.
You fell asleep reading and woke up in the dark.

You could almost see your face along the far wall
in the armoire's mirrored door
and squinted as if a light—as if to look across
a great distance. On the bedside table: your watch,
your wallet and keys—where you left them.

Letter from the Cumberland

I live among the nameless birds, gunshots at dusk.
The ferry's lamp sways from bank to bank
as if in search of someone lost. From the porch
I watch it pass, the trees lit. Walking up the drive—
the tiny stones, the evening's songless air—
I wonder where it stops. I can't say,
though the boxes have been broken down for months,
the pictures hung, my name exchanged with neighbors.
We wave across the street. They nod from the mailbox.
They don't ask much. I settle in, wind my clock.

To Orpheus

It isn't madness but shame for wanting
and shame for not having what I want,

which is a kind of madness—drunk,
3 a.m., the stairwell too steep to climb.

The bed can wait. I go to the pool instead,
strip and step in, the smell of smoke and sweat

washing from hair and skin. The wet kiss:
his mouth pressed here, my neck, and there,

my chest—in the end—went nowhere.
Cars pass with coupled strangers. I wade.

The brick wall stretches into the sky,
the sky empty, save the constellations,

whose lives I love—yours most of all,
father of poets, whose lyre filled trees

and stones with awe, the lover torn to shreds
and thrown into the river. Tonight,

you're the swan, lost among pinholes of light,
your throat bitten by a black hole

that takes and takes and never fills. I kick,
stroke my tired arms to buoy this body.

It makes ring after perfect ring, but each one
breaks along the edge. You who never were,

did you look down on the world at last
and see that more won't be enough? Not now.

Not ever. Want picks the human heart.
You're the lie I won't believe forever.

A Definition of Terms

1. Cruise, as in, *I didn't plan to cruise*
anyone: a verb, slang, to seek a trick,
usually at night; no connection to
Tom Cruise, beloved actor and movie star.
2. Trick: a noun, slang, a.k.a. "good-love,"
"one-night stand"; a verb, to have sex

with someone of the same or opposite sex,
the number of which often accrues
with increased loneliness and lack of love.
That's what we became, two potential tricks
that morning at the airport, co-stars
in some fantasy, the story of two

strangers, their flights delayed, waiting to
board their planes. You watched me. You: a sexy
Spaniard dressed in black, save the All Star
tennis shoes (nice touch). Bored, I watched planes cruise
the runway, drew the same geometric
shape in my book: *circle, circle*. . . . but I love

the fear that comes with desire, and I love
to be desired, so though I thought, *No, it's too*
early, not a chance, I'm too tired to trick,
and *Where the hell would we have sex*
anyway, before long I was the one cruising
you, the idea of us, a fleck of light, a star

growing brighter. I walked past you, star-
ing at you with a smile, as if to say, *I'd love*
to get it on, passengers and flight crews

too busy fighting or sleeping or gabbing to
see what we were up to, see us talking sex
without talking. You followed me. We tricked

them all. An hour later, I'm alone. My plane tricks
the pull of gravity, taking me home, star-
ward, as the ground grows and grows. The sex
was great: a bathroom stall, a soft love-
grip, buckles, buttons, good-bye kiss, all too
fast to forget, tender to confuse. 1. To cruise:

to seek comfort in a body. 2. Trick: the cruised,
the lonely, the starved; sex between strangers
who give and take this temporary love.

In the Absence of Love, the Heart Seeks a Constant

The bluff endures, for now, despite April winds.
It loosens, stone by stone, the landslide slow
and imperceptible. At night the city becomes

a sea of stars blinking, minor constellations:
they have their tales to tell. My porch lamp joins
the many, plays its part. How? I cannot know

from here, below the cliff, among yellow lawns
and sprinklers. The slightest step outside—my cat
or neighbor stumbling home—triggers the light.

It splashes the still life in my window: two cups
stacked in the sink, a lime, knife, and cutting board.
The bluff holds. Down the hall someone is sleeping.

Letter from the Cumberland

They lived nearby, I was in the book, and what kind of name was
 ----,
anyway? My students blinked in the porch light. One day
they want to teach in town, having lived here all their lives.
They knew everyone: even the dregs at the liquor store,
the pregnant girl down the road, *niggers*, though not by name.
Their words rippled out, far from them, over the town
with its thousand steeples. Behind me, my family held
their poses in their tiny frames, each of us a shade lighter than
our parents. On the wall, my mother frowned, her closed mouth
about to break. When I left she said, *Don't tell them who you are*.
And once, you warned, *More people want us dead because we're fags*.
I closed the door and watched them shift behind the screen.
I hated them. I hated them for all of us, though no one asked me to,
and wished them a lesson in pain. It wasn't right, but I didn't care.

A Story of Winter

The ice breaking, and a circle of trees
around the lake. Skates laced
and unlaced. A boy with blue mittens.

His sister, that winter: hot soup
and a spoon skimming the bottom.
Outside, a scarf, a red coat, snow

and more snow—then less. Day and night,
the lake freezing and thawing,
the mittens, the heavy skates.

The laces woven and knotted twice.
Ice breaking. A circle of trees
waving branches. A spoon skimming

the bottom. Day and night:
a crystal bottle on the table,
a room painted white, the candles lit,

a curtain drawn. Outside, snow
and more snow, an empty field,
a lake breaking. And night

after night, a piano or someone singing.
A velvet dress, a pressed collar,
a string of pearls. More snow,

then less. Inside: a black band
in her brown hair, and candlelight
along the walls, wavering. Like water.

Like light on water. And the boy.
There. Then not there.
The ice breaking. The heavy skates

skimming the bottom. His sister's coat
in the closet among the many coats.
A mother's hands in her lap. The song

spilling out. A father and his scotch.
Für Elise. A circle of trees.
Their mouths shut. The heavy skates.

The youngest taken to bed.
That winter. The ice breaking.
The room full of song and no one speaking.

Snow and more snow. Then less.
The youngest led away.
The air changing over and over again.

Homage

for my brother

Face down on the warm wood of the pier,
fingers between the planks, I was a lizard.

Below the surface a blowfish grew
into a globe. The teeth on its back rose,

drawing poison to the tips. You worked
the lip of a paper cup. You tore and ripped,
tore and bent it into a boat

that could only last a moment
between the splashes.

Snow on snow. It sealed the front door shut.
We waited until it thawed below our bedroom window.

You dressed me in layers.
I followed (an untied lace) across the yard,
our boots crunching boot-tracks in the snow.

We buried ourselves in the woods
until silence nestled itself between us.

Only the pines could shake
the heaviness off their needles.

The older one, you took me out of the house.
We crossed the yard—
blades of grass brushed against our bare feet.

(I thought they could color us in.)
We rarely talk now, but I haven't forgotten
our quiet walks under the dim light of streetlamps.

It is all kept, a stone, inside.

Tonight, a half moon.
Its missing side grows in my mind.

Waterborne

We tipped it so often the rudder broke
close to shore, but we drifted, asking:
How deep? I imagined columns of stone:
Someone would come. Someone always came,
but the hill where Mother sometimes stood
seemed to sink, and the sea grew harder.

To Know You Better

I sleep in the bed you were born in.
Vines of passion fruit strangle the house,
and trees your father planted
still bear their inedible fruit. The taste
is in the leaves, you always said.

The stump in the backyard
must have been the almond tree
where you chained your dog.
And when you left, they say,
the dog walked into the hills,

chain dragging from its neck.
Men gather for the cockfight,
crowd shoulder to shoulder,
but I can still see the birds,
their wings too large for their bodies,

sweeping the ground like small brooms.
At a table, men lower their faces,
dominoes cupped in their dark hands,
each one a secret.
Women burn palms on the beach,

sell fried fish and plantains in bunches.
They tell me nothing.
They recognize your sway in my walk,
Mother, and their heads
are heavy with disappointment.

What We Have

1.

The son sits at his bedside.
The father hears a violin.
Can you hear it? When it strikes
the final chord, he turns

to face his son: *I don't*
know you. And his son does.
There. The last note
and the absence of that note.

2.

The son, a father, too,
plays chess with his boy.
He tells him how his father died.
The child moves his knight

again. It draws the letter L
across the board, as if
to spell a word
like *love* or *loss*, and fails.

3.

The Expulsion hangs on the wall.
Adam hides his face in his hands.
The boy, a man now,
stands in the bathroom mirror,

still a son. He'll never have
his own. The faucet leaks.
He has this face, these hands,
each drop and the ghost of each drop.

Letter from the Cumberland

You pace the attic of your house, an hour
ahead of me. You pause, pivot, and turn
before the stairs. I'll fly north. You'll drive down
when the time is right. A question mark
over the month of May, months from now.

Want

He is born on a rainy afternoon. Voices ring, lights shine too brightly, and he never forgets the feel of the first hand lifting him up. He cries as women wash him in lavender soap and water, and wrap him in linen.

His mother names him after the men in her life: her father, her brother, and those (she thinks) to come: his son and his son and so on and so on. She listens to the rain, and he, pressed to her chest, hears it pooling inside. The sky grows bright, then dark, then bright for years.

Lying in bed dreaming, he thinks: *Perhaps one day. Perhaps*. He wants it all or wants to fall asleep and wake up wanting less. When it rains, he listens as rivers run from gutters into the garden. And it is almost enough to know that his mother, surely lying awake elsewhere, or the stranger pressed against him in the dark, is hearing it, too.

The Feast of St. John

San Juan, Puerto Rico

We gather at midnight, hundreds of us,
bearing flowers, fruit, or coins to toss
into the sea. Drunk and tired from the trip,
I strip and join the faithful. Cops ride
horses along the beach. We must look
like clumsy ghosts, bare, staggering out

into the dark. We step through foam,
then surf, until we reach the calmer side—
the shells ground to grain. One by one,
the sinners sink, as if his very palm
weighed them down, a thousand miracles.
I float. I rock awhile beneath the sky,

black and boundless. When I stand into
the open air again—revived, not blessed—
among the sanctified, I stumble up
the shore to find my empty cup, my shoes
and shirt, crumpled in the sand—not much,
I guess. They're dry. I'm cold and wet.

The Fear of Being Known

At the market among tables draped with nets,
fishermen and wives haggle for the day's catch.

A knife swings. The blade strikes
the cutting board, scraping heads and tails

to the floor. A hose will wash it clean,
but the air still pools with the smell of rot.

Tree frogs, concealed in a throng of leaves,
hold still. Tonight they'll sing their one song.

Till then, each is a heart,
beating too fast for its own good.

A Ride in the Rain

The driver has no knife. He has no knife, no,
you think, and lower your head into his car.
A ride in the rain? The dark clouds bellow.
You saw him drinking at the local bar,

you think, and lower your head into his car.
Rain taps the roof, falls on this familiar man:
You saw him drinking at the local bar.
He shrugs and offers up his empty hands.

Rain taps the roof, falls on this familiar man,
and sugarcane stalks bend in the breeze.
He shrugs and offers up his empty hands.
As sewer pipes burst, flooding the street,

and sugarcane stalks bend in the breeze,
machetes swing into the green stems, low.
As sewer pipes burst, flooding the street,
bile is a blade at the back of your throat.

Machetes swing into the green stems, low.
A ride in the rain? The dark clouds bellow.
Bile is a blade at the back of your throat.
The driver has no knife. He has no knife, no.

A Call from Whitman Walker Clinic

My grandfather's death was slow and unremarkable.

Someone drew the curtain to let in light,
a vase of tulips stood on the bedside table,
a neighbor sent a basket of cheese and jams,
which he couldn't eat.

The cause was clear: cancer spread
from pancreas to the liver and lungs.

I imagined it growing,
bursting like a pod
to expel the handful of burrs
into the bloodstream—
they traveled a great distance before sticking.

His wife fed him, changed him,
rubbed his lean body down
with a soft cloth and a cake of soap
that held the faint scent of honeysuckle.

The symptoms? Nausea, fever, delirium.
(He didn't recognize his own son, my father.)

I was young and thought there would be
more dignity—no, not dignity, romance,
the way the death of a saint is romantic:

St. Sebastian,
                                        arms bound,
eyes soft in acceptance of the fact,
but his mouth—.

Yesterday, a call from my lover—
The *I'm so sorry* or pause just after
told me what he couldn't.

Because in such cases apologies are useless.
Because there is no room for blame in our lives.
The weight of silence replaces the feathery weight of speech.

In that body,
given with the generosity it takes to love someone,
there is a fury of white seeds,

and each embrace—what loss!—
becomes an opportunity, a question of probability.

A nick? A cut? A scrape? A scratch?

Imagine the second of contact, blood to blood—
how easy! the one small cell slips by,
multiplies exponentially

(simple mathematics, really)—
but this, this is the blood of a body without a face.

I'm aware
of each gesture my body makes,
as if it were someone else's.
This I can be sure of:

I am leaning back in a chair;
the nurse ties a rubber strap to my arm
to slow the surge of blood—
a pinch and I
am spilling into a corked vial.

After my grandfather died,
they adjusted his arms and legs,
turned his head
to transform his knotted body
into one that slept.

In his last few weeks
his pain grew,
he spoke less, was less
a part of our world, slipped
into some corner of his mind—

there was no room for us,
sunlight, or even,
among the tulips beside him,
the smallest blossom
that pinched shut,
refusing to open.

Letter from the Cumberland

As if this were the last light left for miles,
they come, the sky too dark to cross alone.
I stand at the kitchen sink and watch
moths beat against the bright glass. It's late.
My neighbor's door shuts in its warped jamb.
I understand this much: each heavy step
down the iron stairs. I whisper one word
to the air, flick the light. The moths disperse.

Never

But Peter declared, "I will never leave you."

I see that far: next week in empty pockets,
next month in coins scattered on a bed
beside a ring. Once, I fell and hit
my head. I opened my eyes and couldn't see.
Then, I could. Not before my mother sang
softly in my ear, *Okay, okay*, but she
wasn't sure. She squeezed my hand in her hands.
How much the gesture wants to say—.

This is how it will happen: one voice
over many. The constellations shifting above.
Nothing else will matter. Not the men.
What they say or what you say.
It won't count. It won't mean a goddamn thing.
You'll save yourself. Understand? Yourself.

This

He tries to say, *Stop. Stop talking*, but can't,
and you can't, and he is shaking his head,
sobbing. The trees blur into one green wall,

and you can't recall what it was
you couldn't not say. You think, *When we stop,*
he'll get out. We'll never speak again.

You touch his thigh, and he doesn't move.
Everything sighs a little. *What is this?*
He asks, softly now, and studies your face.

He knows and you know what this is and why,
but you can't say, not yet, and he is still
looking at you, and the road goes on and on.

Dear Friend

X.

Your bags were packed
and left at the door, the vase you
filled with shells, wrapped in tissue,
your books boxed. I have the whelk

you found on shore, the small conch,
intact—the point, the fine grooves—
and keep it in a box with a picture of you
at the beach: your hair slicked back,

head cocked at an angle.
Behind you, the green jacket
you told me to throw away. Strewn

over a chair, its arms dangle
above the floor—a hole in the pocket,
the elbows thin from years of use.

Y.

I become each day more reckless,
too impatient for summer, the unbearable heat,
the calm that comes with it. There are no hills here,
not one, and I'm bored with the stillness

of the yellow field outside my window. And you,
who cannot keep still, who can never
look back, where will you go next?
How will I find you?

Can you feel the world pull
apart, the seams loosen?
What, tell me, will keep it whole,

if not you? if not me?
Send a postcard, picture, tell me
how you've been.

Z.

Running down the stairwell in the garden,
I divide the steps by three, until my
foot catches the edge, wet with rain, and my
frame, flung forward by its own momentum,

leans into the night as if reaching
for something I didn't know I
wanted. Not the moon. No. Not the sky,
suspended and limitless. Not even

the tulips standing on their stems
(their petals cup the air).
But in the streetlamp's circle of light, I land

among them, broken.
My body can't contain
itself, as blood burgeons in my hands.

Letter from the Cumberland

I consider the wing and size, the fuss they make
before I give each one a name. I spent the day
watching them dart into trees. In the street
a boy rode his bike around a possum: face up,
its teeth, clean and sharp. Two of its young
crawled from the pouch and got this far.
A bird stood over the dead. Soon there will be
nothing more than a tuft of hair, a clawed foot,
and the name of the one who left them there.

What You Know

Did you know him?

We waited under the awning
for the rain to stop.
He wore a white shirt, jeans.
He wore his hair short.

Did you know him?

He didn't say a word,
silence making him more
than he could ever be.
The stream leaning into the curb
washed everything away.

What did you know?

I knew the rain would stop.
I knew he wouldn't say why,
only, *I can't,*
but I guessed knowing.

What did you know?

I knew when he came back
he wouldn't stay long,
knew, even while he slept,
I did not know him.

Love, then?

Leaning over me in bed
in mid-kiss, he said so,
so the first time he said it,
his mouth moving over mine,
we said it together.

Love, then?

The first time I saw
the statue of Antaeus,
his body in the arms
of another man,
I thought it was love.

And now?

We haven't spoken in years.

And now?

I know he was crushing him.

Simile

She fried steak in vinegar and onions, thumbed a fork into the meat, and licked her fingers, but on nights like this, I cook it rare, so blood seeps out like water from a sponge. Rain batters the window like fingernails tapping the old kitchen table. And thunder shakes like cars crashing or a chair tipping over on its side or bottles breaking on the sidewalk. When lightning strikes, I think of her childhood home: candied guava and goat cheese, the smell of warm wood on the docks, tree frogs singing, her stories so large, they were like cardboard boxes one could sleep in. Sitting at the foot of my bed, she'd whisper about grass dolls and flower chains and the dog she tied to the almond tree in her yard. The dog stashed its puppies in the tall grass. Her father tied them up in a shoebox and threw them into the river. We'd pray, *Padre Nuestro*, and then to the Virgin softly, *Dios te salve, María, llena eres de gracia*. She cracked the bedroom window during storms and said the air sweetened like sugarcane fields. She'd steal a machete and cut a stalk or two, hide at the foot of the mountain that sheltered the town from hurricanes. Once, when I heard someone pacing outside the bedroom door, the smell of burnt steak in the air, she told me about fishermen's boats in the bay, how they whined like floorboards when waters were rough. Tonight, she'd say, the rain ticks like coffee beans stirred over the embers, pockets of smoke and vapor rising, like leaves rattling on stems, or this steak left sizzling on the stove, grease spitting up from the pan. The timer he bought. It wound and ticked as fast as a bomb.

And Though We Know It Does No Good

All morning, *changos*
cross the yard. Otherwise,

a lizard on the branch—
his throat, a red balloon.

And at the bottom of the hill,
a boy. Surely, the bus

has come and gone.
(This has nothing to do

with her.) Meanwhile,
the clouds won't give.

The roosters won't
stop crying.

Someone says, *Sirena*, and
you know the word

from the story she told
slowly, without anger: *Why*

my skin, lifting her sleeve—
Look—a finger in the air

to say, *Listen*. Then
pointing out the window—

Over there, for hours
in the sun—where she'd swim.

They said, *You'll grow fins*
and won't come back.

Which is what it means.
Which is what happened.

From shore they saw
her sink—a girl.

What does it matter now
if her dress hung on a branch

or bloomed about her?
And who is left to say?

She lies on a bed across the sea.
This was well before

the pier was built or washed away,
plank by plank. The wind—

you can almost hear
the wind. They must have called

her name. They must have called
and called her name.

Benediction

From the porch we can see the foothills of Cayey.
I carried you here in my arms.

Mother's nervous in the kitchen, washing plates
in the sink. She brings a slice of cake.

She brings a glass of water, begging you to drink.
Mother, she says, *who am I?* You nod or shake your head.

She lifts the shoulder of your dress,
which falls below your collarbone.

The rest is nonsense.
The mountains will never be mountains again.

Elegy

She tossed a key from the second floor
onto the street. You let yourself in
and made your way up the flight of steps,
dark and narrow. This is important:
You moved slowly and afraid, a hand
on either wall. Out there, a choir sang.
The window was open, and the difference
between the two became difficult
to understand: the night sky and the air
inside or one day from the next.
You had lit votives to watch the chapel shimmer
and didn't pay a dime. Upstairs,
she waited with a photo, another story,
a book of poems she wanted you to read.
Julia de Burgos lived here once,
years before the river and the unmarked grave.
They buried her within twenty-four hours.
When you arrived, months later,
you weren't sure: She was already gone.
The dark opened up into more darkness.

Letter from the Cumberland

You wouldn't
the years I begged. Would
the years I wouldn't.
—Sandra Cisneros

A crow fell over a field of tall grass,
one wing flapping against its body
uselessly, and I recalled your question:

Even if I would, could you?

But first,
I never thanked you for books you sent
wrapped in gold tissue and green ribbon.

They arrived at my door open, but
I saw the bits of tape and paper left
behind.

The answer is yes. Each night
I fly back home, repeating the word—
If. If.—from your last letter.

I look
to the cliff where a bronze bird leans
over the edge, tipped wings spread
as if it could.

The Vanishing Point

She'd seen maps and could name the nearest island,
which I couldn't see,

my eyes fixed on the farthest wave.
Boys carried a mutt to the end of the pier,

pushed it over the edge,
and threw stones at its head

as it struggled to shore. They found
their mark again and again and again.

I held her hand with both hands.
The dog sank,

and the boys walked away,
dumping rocks from their pockets.

The last night I saw her,
years later, frying onions in a large pan,

her arms were sleeved in steam and oil.
I was talking about the dead, and she nodded,

immune to the vapors, as if she thought
I was onto something but couldn't help,

her hands so slick they'd glisten under any light.
That day I thought, *It's there*,

though I couldn't see the dog—
and think of it down there still.

The Autopsy

The smell was a curtain I moved through. A woman was stretched on a table, her chest peeled back, her body a sack too large for its contents. Some of her parts were piled beside her, her face loose, breasts almost touching the table on either side. A ladle spooned blood from the bowl of her body, and her mouth hung open as if to speak. *I bet you didn't know*, the man holding the knife said, breathing deeply, *that blood smelled so sweet*. He sliced the heart he held in his hand, when my head began to sway, and I stepped drunk to the open window—the air, water splashing over me. The darkness closed in, the men with white aprons laughing. The odor followed me for months, a child asking questions, insisting, in the cafeteria or train station—the woman with her wooden bowl. She was old, bent like someone clearing her throat. As I walked away, she shook the bowl of change in her hands, her perfume spreading down the hall, the scent of sweet lavender.

Prayer

If night covers the room,
taking everything away,
the difference between
this and that, all sense of edge,
mark, or sign of life,

and there is no ceiling to stare into,
no walls where shadows rise,
no center, no balance, no line,
no book, photo, or sunflower's face
fanning yellow petals

(circles inside brown circles)—
not even that—
and the moon refuses to play its part,
shutting its one dead eye,
and there is no sleep, no dream,

no glass of water on the bedside table,
no bedside table,
let light come,
so night's lost cup of peppermint tea
for nerves, for sleep,

held tightly in my hands
and set down somewhere in that awful dark—
let it and all the rest,
in time and shape,
become themselves again.

The Muse

When the mountains caught on fire,
I didn't dance in a city of witches.
It didn't rain. I peeled mangos,
fallen and skin-torn. There were no
orange hearts. I picked leaves to boil
till clouds of amber spread in water,

not omens, not signs of storms to come.
I lit fires on shore, unafraid
of the wood and crab shells that cracked
and hissed at my fingertips. My skin
burned. I threw my gloves at men,
found sugar in the cane, and they

came from the hills and the bay.
I never mended nets, and if I did,
my needle didn't jump in and out
of the cloth like a dolphin. It didn't jump.
When they returned, their boats full
of silver, I had nothing to do with it.

To Useless Things

He was a freak. Fucked from the start. A child,
he hoarded shoes he outgrew, treasured shards
of a broken plate, chaff, the piece of yarn
his sister drew from her scarf. He prized

the useless, the forgotten, the left-behind:
a burnt bulb, a sock, a leash and collar,
the gold band buried (smell of copper)
deep in a jar of pennies. Now, his vice

is a glance, a scrap of voice, touch, slow strokes
and a *You, yes, you*, till he grows hard
in someone's hand. He's let so many men

do this, what's one more? He nods, *Let's go*.
It's enough to make his whore of a heart
drum its blood, beat two words: *love them, love them*.

Letter from the Cumberland

The river's risen since you left. It moves
(but doesn't seem to move) along the cliff,
the houses on its edge. The birch in back
has lost its leaves. What else? The pines. The rain.
And five deer, in full view, across the lawn.
(At once, they leapt into the woods as if—)

Then, of course, the bird—you'd know what kind—
stuck in the chimney shaft. All night I heard
its feathers brush the brick, and when it stopped,
its still wing stretched, I pulled it from the flue.

They leapt as one into the woods, but first,
they stopped. I stopped. We stood like this
a long time. I thought, *It must be cold*
in Amherst now. And then, *Someone has to give*.

In the Garden: After

Dawn or just before. The rainy season spills
into the next with all its wind.

The fruit's fallen, the speckled skin split,
and tree frogs sing the same wordless question.

The only answer is
the question they ask and ask all night.

This is longing. For more. For something else.
You learn to live with it.

Elsewhere

The storm lit the room with a blue, fluorescent flash.
Even the dog stared into the darkness for some time
after, wide-eyed. In the morning, mist sprays the car
on the way to work, as tobacco barns pour sweet smoke

over the street, the pond where cows circle, and
you wonder if what could have been
was ever waiting for you
somewhere. You rest your head against the glass.

The deer dragged from the edge of the road isn't waiting
for anyone, though you look for it each day you pass.
You'd like to walk into the damp field where its legs
rise stiffly through the tall grass, the color of tall grass.

The Perfect Hour

The dog empties his lungs in one long sigh.
The cat stops to join the room's stillness.
After this. And before the phone begins
to miss the sound of its bells. Then. I do
not want. No sip of water. No wool socks,
despite the first frost or deep, cold night.
No one. Not even for the hour to last
longer than it might.

Beyond This

A train plows through a field of sunflowers,
and though clouds form a thin veil,
the yellow faces follow the sun's arc.

In the distance, a group of boys circle a tree.
They laugh aloud and thrust their skinny arms
into the thicket.

Cherries, you think,
and slowly turn the word over your tongue
so it comes out weighted and real as a pit.

Behind them, a row of cottonwoods bloom,
their seeds spreading through the air,
and if memory serves you right,

the town
bustles just beyond, where women and men
carry meats, fish, and fruit from the market,

and church bells ring. Somewhere
a wife cracks a dry poppy's bulb—
seeds flavor the morning bread,

the way her husband likes it. Somewhere
a gold band turns in a man's hands,
drops into a bowl of cold peach soup—

he pinches his ring below the running water
but days later says it still sticks to the skin.
What if you could see that far or farther?

See past the farm dotting the hill,
where a man sharpens his knife
to kill the winter pig. Where two girls

sneak down the cellar steps to drink
the last of the raisin wine. What if
you could see beyond this? Beyond shore and sea—

What then? Past the sky? Past the moon,
whose yellow-tinted head hangs over you
          both round and heavy in the air?

Not There

The sun is everywhere, but my neighbor doesn't mind.
She kneels in the flowerbed, a floppy hat,
a small shovel in her gloved hand. When she stops,
she leans in the door to catch her breath,
her head bare and bald. Once, my mother held
her breast to show us where they cut the tenderness
away. She sank into a pillow and fell asleep,
but I looked around the room for something
that wasn't there, which is what she wanted us
to see—the not-there, a black star stitched
over the heart. Like the bird that broke her neck
against the window. Her wings, green and iridescent,
were beautiful and useless. The joints moved
like the links of a chain, a bracelet or necklace draped
across my fingertips—and bile spilled from her beak.
Until then, I thought she might live. I often know
when the dog is at the door, before he barks.
And when I call, my mother always says,
I was thinking of you. At dusk, the neighbor's husband
waters the ground beneath the blossoms, but
he doesn't do it for them. A dark grows
over the street as it begins to rain, as it begins
to pool and flood. Another day ends.
Every morning, down the hill, the hammers bang
for hours, and treetops sway. Soon enough,
we'll see what they've been building all along.

Hubble's Law

Before dawn, fishermen motor far into the open sea.
The bay long dead. Their lanterns lit.

Meanwhile, in the plaza, the manicured trees
strung with lights, the fountain and its expanding rings.
The steeple. The brown, plaster Christ.
Yellow mountains rise in the background,

and the houses are sleeping. I sit at the window
and think of a dock stretching in darkness,
my hands, a net cast: it opens and opens wider,
the weights never breaking the surface, never sinking.

Beyond the pier, the lights disperse,
each a star beneath the stars, a boat, a man drifting out.

Perihelion

And it is brighter, clearer, the hangers robed
with winter coats, the cat at the open window.

The breeze breaks a stillness
that fell on the house weeks ago,

and everything seems full of its own potential
again, like a thin reed or taut string, a hammer.

In the photo, my grandmother presses a finger
to a glass globe—birds in a snow flurry—

and looks as if she's on the verge...
like her Lladró figurine, who knows what she wants—

a porcelain hand grasping at blue stems.
There is a story: a hummingbird and the one

hibiscus he searches for. How tired
his wings must be. Light falls through the glass.

A figure climbs the steps. A red scarf.
It's the way, standing at the stove,

I stir, the spoon warming in my hand.
First, I don't notice. Then it's too hot to hold.

The Battle of Nashville

Snow gives the sky a new dimension—depth,
a soft glow, as if the air lit the yard,
which slopes to the city, which shimmers.
The river is always moving, but the atrium
on Fifth, the Kress, where blacks locked arms
and would not budge. A plow takes the hill,
where cars line up in rows, and half-built lofts
replace the houses. The man who built our house
built diesel engines, and kept the trucks
he couldn't fix. His daughters sold it all,
except the how-to books, the shop fan
he left in the attic. We're not brave,
but we find each other in bed at night,
your hand or my hand reaching out.
In the morning, you take the trash, I make
the coffee. Nearby, battles were fought,
and men, whose wives waited for them, died.
If soldiers held the highest ground, one stood
here. If there is one, there is at least
one more. Standing shoulder to shoulder,
they share a blanket, as snow settles in the trees.
I think they are afraid. I think this is love.

A Question of Gravity and Light

You swept a broom into the dustpan I was holding.
Pulverized, you said, *diamonds in the floorboards,*

which was what I thought,
diamonds, as I knelt beneath the bare, bright bulb.

In the ceiling, a broken bolt.
The bronze fixture had fallen on the tabletop,

and both had shattered:
a spray of black and smoky glass.

Days later we found shards flung across the couch—
What if I—What if you had been—

and set our plates on the floor.
That night we hauled the table to the barn.

We can fix it, you said, though I wasn't sure we would.
You ran back to the house. The rain

silvered beneath the lamppost, the rain
showered you in cold drops of light.

I stood among blue tarps and boxes,
a hammock full of leaves. A plane flew overhead.

A dog rooted through the far field,
his tail in the air. It was onto something.

You were almost there.
And I hurried after you.

Epilogue

To the Reader

She stands on the rocks in high heels. She looks
out of place, meaning elegant: a silk scarf
in her hair, a string of pearls, the sea nudging
the shore relentlessly. The photographer winds
and leans into the shot—the story still to come—

in English, of course. Who'd have guessed: a girl
like her from a town like this. . . . The stones
wobble under her weight. A shell cracks. She points
to a hook. Click. The shoes are a lie. The scarf,
a lie. The pearls. Click. Fishermen blush, but

the rest is true—their daily exchange, and more
than half of what she says. Look at her now.
A boy is climbing the tallest tree, a blade tied
to his belt. Below, girls lift their hands into the air.
The bay full of boats. They've come all this way.

Acknowledgments

Some of these poems, or versions of them, first appeared in the following journals: *Bellevue Literary Review*, *Cimarron Review*, *Crab Orchard Review*, *Cranky Literary Journal*, *Cream City Review*, *Full Circle Journal*, *Green Mountains Review*, *The Grove Review*, *Indiana Review*, *The Lyric Review*, *New Delta Review*, *Phoebe*, *Poet Lore*, *Puerto del Sol*, *River City*, *Southern Poetry Review*, *The Texas Review*, *Third Coast*, and *Washington Square*.

For their support, I would like to thank Daniel Blasi, Michael Blumenthal, Yvonne Boustany, Judith Broome, Juan Buono, Joseph Cassell, Lisa D. Chavez, Marisa Clark, Jean Howden, Jessica Grant-Bundschuh, Antonio Jocson, Elline Lipkin, Beth Martinelli, Helena Mesa, and June Yang. Special thanks to the Center of Excellence for Creative Arts at Austin Peay State University, and to the editors at the University of Arizona Press for their generosity. Also, my family and teachers.

About the Author

Blas Falconer completed his MFA at the University of Maryland and his PhD at the University of Houston. He has received several awards for his poetry, including the Associated Writing Programs Intro to Journal Award, the Academy of American Poets Prize, and the Barthelme Fellowship. He teaches at Austin Peay State University in Clarksville, Tennessee, and is the poetry editor for *Zone 3* magazine and Zone 3 Press.